I0159363

Testimonials

Heart

"I've always known God loves me, but my heart never believed it. When my world fell apart, and I was abandoned, God's love overtook me. As He put together the broken pieces of my life, the connection between my heart and mind was finally made."
Cary Sanchez, Speaker, Author, Blogger www.CarySanchez.com

"In the pain, hurt, and heartbreak of life, tender love steps in--the forever-love of a faithful Father and kind King. He wraps us in strong arms and holds us close to show again and again that He is here. And it is enough."
Beth Saadati, Writer, Teacher www.bethsaadati.com

Soul

"When I surrendered my life to Christ, my soul was changed forever – I belong to God. He fills me with wisdom beyond my understanding. His grace and mercy were not purchased, but given! God completed my soul by filling me with Him."
Bobbie Frazier www.bobbiefrazier.net.
www.prayerpocketministry.com

"Today's culture beckons us to conform, but God commands us to be transformed. (Read Romans 12:2 in the Bible.) Transformation involves our whole body. It is a surrender of the will, the action of giving up ourselves, and receiving God's fullness. May God's truths renew your mind, body, and soul."
Julie Dykes Out of the Ruins Ministry. Speaker, Singer, Writer.
Helping the broken to the glory of God.

Mind

"Spinning with to-do lists, chaos of life and unfulfilled expectations, my mind was hungry for rest. When I reached out for God, He restored my weary mind with refreshment, renewal and comfort—a priceless gift! In need of hope or restoration? He is waiting to replenish your mind!"
Angela Holston, Speaker, Writer www.AngelaLight.com

"Trust me. Satan is after control of my mind. He is deceptive, disparaging, discouraging, depressing, destructive, and demeaning. But I belong to Christ. I am His, and He is mine. He is the truth, hope, and love."
Jan Willis, Speaker, Writer, Blogger. jankwillis.com @janjkw.

Strength

"I used to think strength was about me, and my ability to act strong through trials. Yet, experience has taught me that true strength is released through an internal calmness that results from a deep faith, unwavering trust, and confidence in the Lord. (Read Ephesians 6:10 in the Bible.)"
Jerri Marr, Speaker, Writer Jerrimarr.wordpress.com

"The Apostle Paul wrote that he would rather boast his weaknesses than his strengths. When we dare to become vulnerable and expose our true self, imperfections and all, that's when we are the strongest. Relationships help expose our blind spots and acknowledging them empowers change."
Naomi R. Shedd Speaker, Blogger, Author. *Pictures with a Purpose, Going from Scrapbooks to Faithbooks* www.unleashedd.com

BOOKS BY MELISSA KIRK

NONFICTION

GRACE WARRIOR DEVOTIONAL SERIES

GRACE WARRIOR – *Bathed in Mercy, Clothed in Grace*

GRACE WARRIOR – *At the King's Command*

ADVENT – *Celebrate the Coming*

...watch for more in the Grace Warrior Devotional Series

GRACE WARRIOR DEVOTIONAL SERIES

The *Grace Warrior Devotional Series* is designed to enhance the reader's relationship with God. Each book in the series stands alone. As a whole, the books in the series build a foundation for kingdom living.

Grace Warrior – *At the King's Command* encourages the reader to focus on spiritual loyalty. This book is especially useful for understanding God's edict concerning your relationship with him.

It begins with a short introduction. From there, it focuses on the topics: Heart, Soul, Mind, and Strength. There are seven sections per subject. Worship reading is first and opens a conversation with God about the topic. The next six readings look at the theme from the perspectives of *Foundation, Acceptance, Belief, Planning, Growing, and Sharing.*

Each reading is short to encourage time for personal interaction with God through his word and prayer. Although numbered for a four-week journey, the reader should dwell on each topic as long as they wish. There is a discussion guide included for those who would like to read and discuss the devotional together.

GRACE WARRIOR

At the King's Command

Grace Warrior Devotional Series

Melissa Kirk

Grace Warrior

GRACE WARRIOR – *At the King's Command*

Published by Charlene Publishing
Copyright ©2015 by Melissa Kirk
Cover Design by oberkromdesign.prosite.com

Charlene Publishing

Scripture quotations are taken from the Holy Bible, New Living Translation, copyright ©1996, 2004, 2007, 2013 by Tyndale House Foundation. Used by permission of Tyndale House Publishers, Inc., Carol Stream, Illinois 60188. All rights reserved.

ISBN-13: 978-0996923125 (Charlene Publishing)
ISBN-10: 0996923128

All rights reserved. No part of this book may be reproduced or transmitted in any form or by any means, electronic or mechanical, including photocopying and recording, or by any information storage and retrieval system, without permission in writing from the publisher.

Published in the United States

First Edition.

To my daughters, Melanie and Ericka.

You shower grace upon me.

♥

May you always be grace warriors.

You are my precious gifts from God.

I love you.

GRACE WARRIOR

At the King's Command

Contents

Excerpts

GRACE WARRIOR –

ADVENT –

GRACE WARRIOR

Her new position is reflected on the cover of this book.

Grace looked at the challenging list. Today she had to be wife, mother, daughter, and boss. Be caring, creative, and – she scribbled across the top of the page – be nice.

She turned to the throne. "How can I successfully serve you with so much to do?"

"Daughter," He said. "I have told you the way. Remember the most important edict, and all will be well."

Grace Warrior bowed in obedience. She was *at the King's command.*

You can see her original position on the book cover of Grace Warrior –*Bathed in Mercy, Clothed in Grace*

GRACE WARRIOR

Definition:
A child of God, who handles Kingdom business with dignity
and determination.

"All of me belongs to God."

The Edict

My mother loves the McIntosh variety apple. She says it's full of flavor, easy to digest, and bakes well. When they're in season, she loads up. I can be sure she will send some home with me because she knows I agree – they are delicious.

What makes it good is everything under its skin. The fruit thrives with a strong core, seed, flesh, and stem. Properly grown and harvested, it's pleasing to the taste buds. Just as God intended.

In similar fashion, everything good about us is under

our skin in impalpable life sources created by God; wholly designed to glorify him. As Christ-Followers, we are a sampling of his perfect flavor.

To enable us to yield the proper taste of his goodness, he issued an edict he calls the most important command.

"And you must love the Lord your God with all your heart, all your soul, all your mind, and all your strength."

Mark 12:30

This is a direct order between him and us which God doesn't trivialize. Our adoption into the kingdom came at the highest cost; the blood of Jesus. To say that he wants all our energy concentrated on all things godly would be wrong. He doesn't want it. He demands it.

The duty appears daunting, but here's the beautiful thing. He *created* our heart, soul, mind, and strength, and knows their full potential. If we yield to his authority, our human limitations cease to matter. God has high expectations and gives us his unlimited, all-powerful grace to overshadow our weaknesses.

We will never be able to fully embrace this command. The closest we come is if we willingly lay ourselves to be martyred. However, he knows we are imperfect people and is not only faithful to put our perceived failed attempts in right standing, but to also use them to bring attention to him.

What's under your skin? Does your heart beat for God? Does your soul reveal you prefer him over everything else? Is your mind calculating every move to benefit the Almighty? Are you using every ounce of your strength to follow his instruction?

It's our call to obedience. Friend, embrace it. God created you. He walks life's path with you. He preserves your life for the number of days he determines right. He's prepared an everlasting home for you. He loves you and has exciting plans for you. He watches over you as the apple of his eye.

Your next breath is dependent on him.

God adds a second command that he says is just as important.

"The second is equally important: 'Love your neighbor as yourself.' No other commandment is greater than these."

Mark 12:31

I believe obeying the second edict will subconsciously happen if we are complying with the first.

With this devotion, my prayer is that Christ-Followers will find the determination to follow God's command by reflecting on his Word.

If you aren't a Christ-Follower, I pray that you will come to an understanding of God's authority and your position with him.

HEART

Definition: where interest thrives

"A divided heart loses both worlds."

A. B. Simpson

Day 1 - HEART

In Worship

Proclamation

Heart

God's heart seeks out the lost to offer them sanctuary. Our refuge is found in Jesus, *God's Son*. I run to his safety through faith in the victory over death by Jesus, *my Savior*.

What does my heart do?

God gave me heart to exercise what my mind perceives to be important. My allegiance is to God's promises. I have set my affections on his will.

How important is my heart?

It opens the way to see God. Read *Matthew 5:8.*

Who sees my heart?

The Lord. Read *Jeremiah 17:10.*

Receiving God's Word

"My heart is confident in you, O God; my heart is confident. No wonder I can sing your praises! Wake up, my heart! Wake up, O lyre and harp! I will thank you, Lord, among all the people. I will sing your praises among the nations. For your unfailing love is as high as the heavens. Your faithfulness reaches to the clouds."

Psalm 57:7-10

Connecting with God's Word

How confident are you in God?

Responding to God's Word

Do you have something you want to say to God about heart?

Heart

What truth about heart can you relate to today?

Day 2 - HEART

The Outpouring

Hannah fought depression, often crying and losing her appetite. Other women taunted her because she was childless. During the time in which she lived, barrenness was a sign of failure or even judgment from the Almighty.

The young Jewish woman took her pain to God and prayed. She made a vow to him that if he gave her a son, she would dedicate the child back.

One day at the Tabernacle, she was in such a sad state that Eli, the priest, thought she was drunk. He questioned her and she replied she was pouring out her heart to God. Then the priest began to encourage her.

God answered her prayer and she gave birth to Samuel, who grew to become a mighty leader. Read *I Samuel 1.*

Like Hannah, God wants us to pour out our heart and then offer everything that he fills it with back to him.

Like Eli, he wishes us to watch for family, friends, and strangers who may be hurting and encourage them.

Receiving God's Word

"Oh no, sir!" she replied. "I haven't been drinking wine or anything stronger. But I am very discouraged, and I was pouring out my heart to the LORD. Don't think I am a wicked woman! For I have been praying out of great anguish and sorrow."

I Samuel 1:15

Connecting with God's Word

Have you ever poured out your heart to God?

Responding to God's Word

Is there anything you want to say to God about your heart?

Heart

What truth about heart can you relate to today?

9

Day 3 - HEART

All In

My Texas sisters, Carmen, Lynn, and Becky, really know how to throw a party. It was my birthday and what a surprise!

The house was decorated luau style. There was even a Tiki Bar for the kids in the backyard. The grill was fired up and the table overflowed with shish kabobs and salads. The display was a huge cocktail glass shaped cake that Becky had baked.

Guests wore leis. They handed me a grass skirt and coconut bra to wear over my regular clothes. The kids wore party hats and coconut bras, too.

The party was in full swing. The little ones danced throughout the living room as the adults laughed and visited.

The chicken and beef shish kabobs smelled wonderful. I helped myself to one and took a bite. It stuck in my throat.

My daughter noticed me first and asked if I was choking.

I nodded.

If a person had to have emergency care, this was a right place and time. There were three nurses and one trained paramedic present.

The party kicked into a different gear.

Someone called 911 while the three nurses took turns doing the Heimlich Maneuver on me, but the piece of meat remained lodged.

Brett, the trained paramedic, took his turn. I think my feet cleared the ground three times, but finally the chunk dislodged.

Everyone was stunned. The house fell quiet except for the baby crying in the bedroom.

As I sat on the back patio trying to regain my composure, the ambulance arrived. The paramedics checked me over and asked if I needed further assistance. I declined.

While signing the release, all my senses rushed back in and I became aware of the surroundings.

My twelve-year-old grandson was tending the Tiki Bar! I suddenly felt an overwhelming need to explain that although we were partying, there wasn't any liquor behind that bar. I blubbered out that it was my birthday surprise, we were all family, and we weren't bothering the neighbors.

"Silly me for choking. Did I mention there's no liquor

at that bar? That's my grandson. He's not – I didn't – Do you want to smell my breath?" I was a blundering mess. (Not remembering if I still had on the coconut bra haunts me to this day.)

They just smiled and shook their heads.

"We love a great party," I told them.

That's how it is when you celebrate with those gals. They're all in. You're all in. And if there's a crisis, your whole heart is in then, too.

That's what God wants for Kingdom work. He wants all his family in, their hearts fully invested. During the good and bad.

Receiving God's Word

"As slaves of Christ, do the will of God with all your heart. Work with enthusiasm, as though you were working for the Lord rather than for people."

Ephesians 6:6b-7

Connecting with God's Word

Do you work for God wholeheartedly?

Responding to God's Word

Is there anything you want to say to God?

Heart

What truth about heart can you relate to today?

Day 4 - HEART

Be Aware

It's important to understand that our heart tends to misguide us in spiritual matters. What we think is right, doesn't always line up with God.

"People may be right in their own eyes, but the LORD examines their heart."

Proverbs 21:2

The Bible gives us instructions on how to ensure our heart correctly guides us. Here are two:

1. The book of Proverbs says that wisdom is found in an understanding heart. Read *Proverbs 14:33.*
2. One Psalm says we should know God's Word in our heart so that we do what is right. Read *Psalm 119:11, 111-112.*

~Heart Knowledge~
Knowing God's words will protect the heart.

Receiving God's Word

"My child, if your heart is wise, my own heart will rejoice! Everything in me will celebrate when you speak what is right."

Proverbs 23:15-16

Connecting with God's Word

How important is it to know what God's Word says?

Responding to God's Word

Is there anything you want to say to God?

Heart

What truth about heart can you relate to today?

Day 5 - HEART

Understand

Receiving God's Word

Do you need God's plan for an obedient heart? "The human heart is the most deceitful of all things, and desperately wicked. Who really knows how bad it is?"

Jeremiah 17:9

Why do you need God's plan for your heart? "But the words you speak come from the heart—that's what defiles you. For from the heart come evil thoughts, murder, adultery, all sexual immorality, theft, lying, and slander."

Matthew 15:18-29.

What is God's plan for your heart? "But I, the Lord, search all hearts and examine secret motives. I give all people their due rewards, according to what their actions deserve."

Jeremiah 17: 10

What is my part in God's plan for my heart? "If you openly declare that Jesus is Lord and believe in your heart that God raised him from the dead, you will be saved. For it is by believing in your heart that you are made right with God, and it is by openly declaring your faith that you are saved."

Romans 10:9-10

Will God's plan for my heart work? "And this hope will not lead to disappointment. For we know how dearly God loves us, because he has given us the Holy Spirit to fill our hearts with his love."

Romans 5:5

How can I know God's plan worked for me? "Let us go right into the presence of God with sincere hearts fully trusting him. For our guilty consciences have been sprinkled with Christ's blood to make us clean, and our bodies have been washed with pure water. Let us hold tightly without wavering to the hope we affirm, for God can be trusted to keep his promise."

Hebrews 10:22-23

Connecting with God's Word

Does God examine hearts? How are you made right with God?

Responding to God's Word

Is there anything you want to say to God?

Heart

What truth about heart can you relate to today?

Day 6 - HEART

The Test

A right heart changes how God watches over us. God protects those who trust him and whose hearts are in tune with him. Read *Psalm 125:1-5.*

A right heart opens communication with God. God speaks to our heart. Read *Psalm 27:8.*

A right heart changes how we see ourselves. We are filled with joy. Read *Psalm 9:1-2.*

A right heart changes our daily focus. We pay attention to where our heart is leading us. Read *Proverbs 4:23.*

Receiving God's Word

"Search me, O God, and know my heart; test me and know my anxious thoughts. Point out anything in me that offends you, and lead me along the path of everlasting life."

Psalm 139:23-24

Connecting with God's Word

Why should we ask God to search our hearts?

Responding to God's Word

Is there anything you want to say to God?

Heart

What truth about heart can you relate to today?

Day 7 - HEART

The Experience

The shepherd boy, David, was referred to by God as "a man after my own heart." *Acts 13:22.*

During his lifetime, he victoriously slew a giant, but later unceremoniously took claim of a married woman. David led the Israelites through massive battles, but also hid in caves and pretended to be crazy. The man murdered, betrayed and rebelled.

As a psalmist, he wrote songs citing his failures and cried out to God for forgiveness. Other times, he sang in victory when God saved him. He hoped to build God's temple.

In the swings of his successes and failures, we find the perfect example of "heart." There's no one more human than David. Yet, he acknowledged God's authority and confessed when he disregarded the Almighty's laws.

With all his imperfections, God appointed him as King of Israel. His story is told in *I Samuel – II Samuel.*

God wants our heart in tune with him in everything, joyful over the victories and repentant over the failures.

Receiving God's Word

"Create in me a clean heart, O God. Renew a loyal spirit within me."

Psalm 51:10

Connecting with God's Word

How would you describe a clean heart?

Responding to God's Word

Is there anything you want to say to God?

Heart

What truth about heart can you relate to today?

Melissa Kirk

Dear Lord,

> *Thank you for examining my heart. Show me my weaknesses and give me your grace to be victorious for you. Create in me the desire to thrive in your perfect will.*

Amen

Melissa Kirk

SOUL

Definition: where relationship is sealed

"The soul becomes dyed with the color of its thoughts"

Marcus Aurelius

Day 1 - SOUL

In Worship

Proclamation

Soul

God determined that my soul is more valuable than any other part of me. I give up my life for the sake of my soul. My life is replaced with Christ, *my Savior*, living in me.

What does my soul do?

God gave me soul to seal my relationship with him. My soul longs for the day where my kinship is fully realized in heaven.

How important is my soul?

It is more valuable than anything. Read *Matthew 16:26.*

Who sees my soul?

The Lord. Read *Proverbs 20:27.*

Receiving God's Word

"If you try to hang on to your life, you will lose it. But if you give up your life for my sake, you will save it. And what do you benefit if you gain the whole world but lose your own soul? Is anything worth more than your soul?"

Matthew 16:25-26

Connecting with God's Word

Do you value your soul as much as God does?

Responding to God's Word

Is there anything you want to say to God about soul?

Soul

What truth about soul can you relate to today?

Day 2 - SOUL

Crying Out

The person who penned Psalm 130 may be unknown to us, but God knows.

The psalmist cried out from the depths of despair. He begged for the Lord to hear as he claimed:

› God keeps no records of wrongs.

› God is the only one we can count on.

› God is to be longed for.

› God is the redeemer.

› God forgives sins.

› God is to be feared.

› God's love is unfailing.

Are loneliness and despair absorbing your soul? You may feel like no one understands or cares.

Look to heaven and cry out to God. He will hear everything you say. You can place your hope in him. Read Psalm

Receiving God's Word

"From the depths of despair, O Lord, I call for your help. Hear my cry, O Lord. Pay attention to my prayer. Lord, if you kept a record of our sins, who, O Lord, could ever survive? But you offer forgiveness that we might learn to fear you."

Psalm 130:1-4

Connecting with God's Word

Have you ever felt like no one cared?

Responding to God's Word

Is there anything you want to say to God?

Soul

What truth about soul can you relate to?

Day 3 - SOUL

Security

While young, I wasn't a fan of fishing. Probably because of the wiggly worms and the hooks that stuck in my foot more times than in the mouth of fish. But I loved Daddy, and he liked to fish.

My father, Edward, insisted I bait my own hook. "Can't catch a fish if you can't bait your own hook," he'd tell me.

After several attempts and words of encouragement from him, I'd finally manage to get a few slips of the hook through the worm. Then, with the pole in hand, I'd head to the water's edge. A few mishaps taught me early on to check for trees and other fishermen before casting into the water.

Daddy thought cane poles and bobbers were best for me. Better for him too. I could tangle line on a reel faster than someone could hand me the pole.

Never able to relax, I'd stare at the round red and white float tilting from side to side, occasionally hiding from me behind the sun's glare. After minutes that seemed like hours, the bobber would pull down and pop back up. My tummy always knotted up. I'd freeze, waiting for the bobber to stop teasing and disappear for good. When it did, I'd yank with all my might.

Hooking a fish didn't happen often, but when I snagged one, Daddy congratulated me.

He was always available to remove the hook from the fish's mouth, which somewhat confused me after him insisting I do everything else. Sometimes the fish was too small and would be thrown back in. That was understandable. But my father had a problem that frustrated me. He had slippery hands. When I caught a good size fish, a lot of times, it slipped out of his grip and flopped back into the water.

His Dean Martin eyes would just squint with an apologetic smile as he handed the pole back and pointed to the tub of worms.

Trips home were depressing because of my slim-to-none contributions to the bucket, but it was always a relief to know that my father wasn't disappointed in me.

The day would end with a good meal. Sometimes it was fish. Other times, it was beans with pork and wilted lettuce or a bologna sandwich with chips and popcorn. Going to bed with a full stomach never depended on the success of the fishing trip.

Years later, I realized Daddy didn't have slippery hands. Turns out I was the chief carp catcher, and Daddy didn't care for carp.

My dad has passed from this earth, but he will always be connected to me through memories; most of him graciously teaching me that failed attempts don't define the day.

Today, my husband and I have a pond that is overstocked with bass. I don't even own a fishing pole. Walking contently by the water's edge is an affirmation that I can't and don't have to do everything well.

I'm reminded that my heavenly Father is my true sustainer. Any effort of mine is dismal and burdensome compared to the expert Fisher-of-Men. God, the Father, has claimed me as his own, and my soul is safe with him. I rest on that promise.

Receiving God's Word

"Then Jesus said, 'Come to me, all of you who are weary and carry heavy burdens, and I will give you rest. Take my yoke upon you. Let me teach you, because I am humble and gentle at heart, and you will find rest for your souls.'"

Matthew 11:28-29

Connecting with God's Word

Do you trust God enough to relinquish your burden and rest your soul?

Responding to God's Word

Is there anything you want to say to God?

Soul

What truth about soul can you relate to today?

Day 4 - SOUL

Be Aware

It's important to understand that our souls become weary when we don't walk with God.

"This is what the Lord says: 'Stop at the crossroads and look around. Ask for the old, godly way, and walk in it. Travel its path, and you will find rest for your souls.' But you reply, 'No, that's not the road we want!'"

Jeremiah 6:16

The Bible gives us instructions on how to ensure our soul remains stable. Here are two:

1. The book of I Corinthians reminds us that we do not belong to our self. God deserves all honor. Read *I Corinthians 6:17-20.*

2. The book of II Corinthians reminds us to live by faith and not sight. Read *II Corinthians 5:1-9.*

~Soul Knowledge~

Knowing God's words will expose the soul's desires.

Receiving God's Word

"But be very careful to obey all the commands and the instructions that Moses gave to you. Love the Lord your God, walk in all his ways, obey his commands, hold firmly to him, and serve him with all your heart and all your soul."

Joshua 22:5

Connecting with God's Word

Have you ever refused to walk God's way? Were you able to rest?

Responding to God's Word

Is there anything you want to say to God?

Soul

What truth about soul can you relate to today?

Day 5 - SOUL

Understand

Receiving God's Word

Do you need God's plan for an obedient soul? "And what do you benefit if you gain the whole world but lose your own soul?"

Mark 8:36

Why do you need God's plan for your soul? "Is anything worth more than your soul?"

Mark 8:37

What is God's plan for your soul? "If you try to hang on to your life, you will lose it. But if you give up your life for my sake and for the sake of the Good News, you will save it."

Mark 8:35

What is my part in God's plan for my soul? "For everyone who calls on the name of the Lord will be saved."

Romans 10:13

Will God's plan for my soul work for me? "Don't be afraid of those who want to kill your body; they cannot touch your soul. Fear only God, who can destroy both soul and body in hell."

Matthew 10:28

How can I know God's plan worked for me? "Now may the God of peace make you holy in every way, and may your whole spirit and soul and body be kept blameless until our Lord Jesus Christ comes again. God will make this happen, for he who calls you is faithful."

I Thessalonians 5:23-24

Connecting with God's Word

Have you asked God to save your soul?

Responding to God's Word

Is there anything you want to say to God?

Soul

What truth about soul can you relate to today?

Day 6 - SOUL

The Test

A right soul changes how God watches over us. God watches and protects those who trust him. Read *Psalm 33:18-22.*

A right soul opens communication with God. God exposes our innermost desires. Read *Hebrews 4:12.*

A right soul changes how we see ourselves. We know God takes care of us. Read *Psalm 63.*

A right soul changes our daily focus. We seek to add souls to the family of God. Read *Proverbs 11:30.*

Receiving God's Word

"There, in a foreign land, you will worship idols made from wood and stone—gods that neither see nor hear nor eat nor smell. But from there you will search again for the Lord your God. And if you search for him with all your heart and soul, you will find him."

Deuteronomy 4:28-29

Connecting with God's Word

Do you think other gods can claim your soul? Why or why not?

Responding to God's Word

Is there anything you want to say to God?

Soul

What truth about soul can you relate to today?

Day 7 - SOUL

The Experience

In the Bible, Jesus talks about the soul after death.

"Finally, the poor man died and was carried by the angels to be with Abraham. The rich man also died and was buried, and his soul went to the place of the dead. There, in torment, he saw Abraham in the far distance with Lazarus at his side. The rich man shouted, 'Father Abraham, have some pity! Send Lazarus over here to dip the tip of his finger in water and cool my tongue. I am in anguish in these flames.' But Abraham said to him, 'Son, remember that during your lifetime you had everything you wanted, and Lazarus had nothing. So now he is here being comforted, and you are in anguish. And besides, there is a great chasm separating us. No one can cross over to you from here, and no one can cross over to us from there.'"

Luke 16:22-26

The scripture emphasis isn't that the poor man went to heaven and the rich man went to hell. The application concerns where their allegiance was while on earth. Who loved God with all their soul?

Receiving God's Word

"But to all who believed him and accepted him, he gave the right to become children of God. They are reborn—not with a physical birth resulting from human passion or plan, but a birth that comes from God."

John 1:12-13

Connecting with God's Word

How do we ensure our soul goes with God after we die?

Responding to God's Word

Is there anything you want to say to God?

Soul

What truth about soul can you relate to today?

Melissa Kirk

Dear Lord,

Thank you for providing security in heaven for those who call on your name. Help me love you completely with my soul. I want to be obedient to your command.

Amen

MIND

Definition: where action is considered

"To see a thing clearly in the mind makes it begin to take form."

Henry Ford

Day 1 - MIND

In Worship

Proclamation

Mind

God speaks his truth in my mind. I place my thoughts under his authority so I can focus on behavior that will reveal his sovereignty and proclaim my salvation through Jesus, *my Counselor*.

What does my mind do?

God gave me my mind to concentrate on things that are noble and praiseworthy. I trust him to lead and protect me.

How important is my mind?

It is where right and wrong is chosen. Read *II Corinthians 10:3-5*.

Who should guide my mind?

The Holy Spirit. Read *Romans 8:5-9*.

Receiving God's Word

"Don't copy the behavior and customs of this world, but let God transform you into a new person by changing the way you think. Then you will learn to know God's will for you, which is good and pleasing and perfect."

Romans 12:2

Connecting with God's Word

Who can change the way you think? What is the result?

Responding to God's Word

Is there anything you want to say to God about mind?

Mind

What truth about mind can you relate to today?

Day 2 - MIND

Searching

King Solomon was both wealthy and wise. Calling himself the teacher, he used his resources to search for the meaning of life and described it as *chasing the wind*. Read *Ecclesiastes 3*.

Here's a brief summary of some of the observations he recorded in the book of Ecclesiastes.

> › Pleasures don't satisfy.
>
> › Work never ends.
>
> › Human wisdom is limited.
>
> › Life isn't fair.
>
> › Talk is cheap.
>
> › The future is unknown.
>
> › Everyone dies.

He ended by saying that everything experienced is meaningless in earthly terms. Yet, God judges everything we do, so obeying him on heavenly terms is our duty.

Receiving God's Word

"That's the whole story. Here now is my final conclusion: Fear God and obey his commands, for this is everyone's duty. God will judge us for everything we do, including every secret thing, whether good or bad."

Ecclesiastes 12:13-14

Connecting with God's Word

Have you ever searched for answers and not found them? How did you respond?

Responding to God's Word

Is there anything you want to say to God?

Mind

What truth about mind can you relate to today?

Day 3 - MIND

One Mind

My grandson, Zakery, has an uncanny ability to draw you into a conversation and build a visual world inside you that is much different than the one you're actually in.

One day, while he was still in preschool, he went with my husband and me to the barber shop. It was a small block building that set just off the highway. A cluster of trees was behind it.

He said, "There's a bear in *them thar* woods."

"There is?"

"Yes. And it's gonna come out to scare us." He thrust his chest out and bared his paws. "And then it's gonna run around the building." He jumped behind the seat and ducked. Shortly, he stretched up to peek out the window.

"What are we going to do?" I asked.

"Not let it get us," he said.

He didn't think any more about his pretend bear, but as we climbed out of the car to go inside, I checked over my shoulder both directions to make sure nothing followed us.

During the last Thanksgiving holiday, Zakery, then fifteen, was our comedian for the evening. His bear story had morphed into a much bigger tale, involving camping and truck beds, and little arms.

He exaggerated the story with hand motions and shirt changes. When he spoke loud, his arms spread wide. Then, as his voice changed to a small squeak, his arms seemed to shrink before our eyes.

The anxieties of life slipped away as we shook our heads and laughed.

I was walking in the field one day when Zakery fell in step with me and put his arm around my shoulders.

"Hey, Mema. You know how you paid Blake when he worked for you last week?"

"Yes. If you need a little money, I have some work you can do."

"I don't want to work. I just thought you might pay me anyway."

I didn't. But, a few weeks later, his mischievous eyes twinkled as he told a long spiel how life was unbearably tough that week. I pulled some money out of my purse and handed it to him.

His eyes grew huge. "You believed that?"

"No. But, you told a good story."

He passionately recreates the fables in his mind. He is so good, people have called to check on his welfare and even thrown him a moving-out-of-town party – when he wasn't going anywhere.

He is always shocked at his audience's response. It amazes him that people believe what he has to say.

His mind is sharp, fast, and calculating. But it is always inclusive. He loves people and is genuinely concerned about the other person's welfare.

I'm not sure what profession he will choose as an adult, but his co-workers are in for a good time.

Positive communication benefits everyone. Stories of victories we've had are perfect opportunities to encourage others that are striving to meet their goals. Trials that we've experienced give us insight that can help someone see their way through a similarly difficult time.

God wants all of us to share our story. If you're wondering what your narrative is, start by asking the Almighty to show you a way to tell about his goodness. It will set your mind on things that matter.

Receiving God's Word

"Is there any encouragement from belonging to Christ? Any comfort from his love? Any fellowship together in the Spirit? Are your hearts tender and compassionate? Then make me truly happy by agreeing wholeheartedly with each other, loving one another, and working together with one mind and purpose."

Philippians 2:1-2

Connecting with God's Word

Do you think you have a story to tell that will help someone?

Responding to God's Word

Is there anything you want to say to God?

Mind

What truth about mind can you relate to today?

Day 4 - MIND

Be Aware

It's important to understand that God doesn't tolerate corrupt thoughts.

"Since they thought it foolish to acknowledge God, he abandoned them to their foolish thinking and let them do things that should never be done."

Romans 1:28

The Bible gives us instructions on how to ensure our mind thinks pure thoughts. Here are two:

1. The book of Colossians instructs us to set our mind on eternal things. Read *Colossians 3:1-16*.
2. The book of Isaiah speaks of the beautiful results from allowing the Holy Spirit to guide the mind. Read *Isaiah 11*.

~Mind Knowledge~
Knowing God's words will separate the truth from lies.

Receiving God's Word

"Avoid all perverse talk; stay away from corrupt speech. Look straight ahead, and fix your eyes on what lies before you. Mark out a straight path for your feet; stay on the safe path. Don't get sidetracked; keep your feet from following evil."

Proverbs 4:24-27

Connecting with God's Word

Where do your thoughts carry you?

Responding to God's Word

Is there anything you want to say to God?

Mind

What truth about mind can you relate to today?

Day 5 - MIND

Understand

Receiving God's Word

Do you need God's plan for an obedient mind? "If we claim we have no sin, we are only fooling ourselves and not living in the truth."

I John 1:8

Why do you need God's plan for your mind? "Those who trust their own insight are foolish, but anyone who walks in wisdom is safe."

Proverbs 28:26

What is God's plan for your mind? "I will put my laws in their minds, and I will write them on their hearts. I will be their God, and they will be my people."

Hebrews 8:10b

What is my part in God's plan for my mind? "And now, dear brothers and sisters, one final thing. Fix your thoughts on what is true, and honorable, and right, and pure, and lovely, and admirable. Think about things that are excellent and worthy of praise."

Philippians 4:8

Will God's plan for my mind work for me? "This is what the Lord says—the Lord who made the earth, who formed and established it, whose name is the Lord: Ask me and I will tell you remarkable secrets you do not know about things to come."

Jeremiah 33:2-3

How can I know God's plan worked for me? "Then you will experience God's peace, which exceeds anything we can understand. His peace will guard your hearts and minds as you live in Christ Jesus."

Philippians 4:7

Connecting with God's Word

What kind of thoughts do you have most often?

Responding to God's Word

Is there anything you want to say to God?

Mind

What truth about mind can you relate to today?

Day 6 - MIND

The Test

A right mind changes how God watches over us. God equips us to do his work. Read *II Timothy 3:17.*

A right mind opens communication with God. God teaches us what truth is. Read *II Timothy 3:16.*

A right mind changes how we see ourselves. We understand that evil wants to control our mind. Read *Romans 7:18-25.*

A right mind changes our daily focus. We allow the Holy Spirit to control our thoughts. Read *Ephesians 4:17-32.*

Receiving God's Word

"He will delight in obeying the Lord. He will not judge by appearance nor make a decision based on hearsay. He will give justice to the poor and make fair decisions for the exploited."

Isaiah 11:3-4

Connecting with God's Word

What types of thoughts control your mind most: evil or good?

Responding to God's Word

Is there anything you want to say to God?

Mind

What truth about mind can you relate to today?

Day 7 - MIND

The Experience

Peter was working when Jesus told the fisherman to follow him and he'd make him a fisher-of-men. Peter's personality showed as he immediately agreed. That's how he was – quick to respond. The Bible gives more than one account of rash decisions that actually got the Christ-Follower in trouble.

A striking example of Peter speaking before processing his thoughts was when he insisted he would never desert Jesus, and even told the Lord he was wrong to think otherwise. That same night, Peter failed to keep his word.

In spite of his missteps, Jesus said the church would grow because of the man's testimony.

Later in life, the disciple warned other believers to guard their minds so they could serve God wisely. Read *Luke 22:31-34, 54-62.*

God created us with unique minds. As Peter, some speak quickly. Others never speak up. Whichever way God made you, he wants your thoughts centered on him.

Receiving God's Word

"Wherefore gird up the loins of your mind, be sober, and hope to the end for the grace that is to be brought unto you at the revelation of Jesus Christ; As obedient children, not fashioning yourselves according to the former lusts in your ignorance: But as he which hath called you is holy, so be ye holy in all manner of conversation; Because it is written, Be ye holy; for I am holy."

I Peter 1:13-16

Connecting with God's Word

Do you try to protect your mind? How?

Responding to God's Word

Is there anything you want to say to God?

Mind

What truth about mind can you relate to today?

Melissa Kirk

Dear Lord,

Thank you for your Word and the Holy Spirit, who give me discernment to know wrong from right. I pray my thoughts will always be pleasing to you.

Amen

Melissa Kirk

STRENGTH

Definition: being intentionally forceful

"You were given this life because you were strong enough to live it."

Author unknown

Day 1 - STRENGTH

In Worship

Proclamation

Strength

God is my strength. I recognize the power and protection he provides. I understand my weakness and accept his grace so that Jesus, *Emmanuel,* can be seen through me.

What does my strength do?

My strength is best demonstrated when I purposefully lay aside my intent to allow God's work to flourish.

Where do I receive my strength?

From the Lord. Read *Exodus 15:2.*

How do I build my strength?

Through the Holy Spirit. Read *Ephesians 3:16.*

Receiving God's Word

"But Lord, be merciful to us, for we have waited for you. Be our strong arm each day and our salvation in times of trouble. The enemy runs at the sound of your voice. When you stand up, the nations flee!"

Isaiah 33:2-3

Connecting with God's Word

How important is God's strength?

Responding to God's Word

Is there anything you want to say to God about strength?

Strength

What truth about strength can you relate to today?

Day 2 - STRENGTH
Misdirected Life

God gave Samson incredible strength, and the Nazirite abused it.

As a young adult, he married into the enemy's family. During the wedding preparations, Samson took a huge risk and lost. He robbed and killed thirty men to satisfy the debt.

Another time, after inciting violence simply because life wasn't going his way, he retaliated by single-handedly killing 1,000 men.

The brutal and reckless lifestyle caught up with Samson. He was captured, tortured and put on display to be humiliated.

The defeated man prayed and asked God to strengthen him just one more time. The Lord answered and with a push of his hands, Samson brought down a building and killed the enemy. Unfortunately, he died too. Read *Judges 13-16*.

It's sad that Samson misused the ability God gave him and suffered. It's interesting that God's objectives were met in spite of his rebellion.

Receiving God's Word

"For who is God except the Lord? Who but our God is a solid rock? God arms me with strength, and he makes my way perfect."

Psalm 18:31-32

Connecting with God's Word

Do you use what God gives you appropriately?

Responding to God's Word

Is there anything you want to say to God?

Strength

What truth about strength can you relate to today?

Day 3 - STRENGTH

Full Focus

Our grandchildren, Ryan and Emercyn, were born thirteen hours apart.

I wasn't able to make it to both birth celebrations, but my husband did. Larry's scramble from one hospital to the other, one hundred thirty miles away, showed his sincere desire to welcome them into the world.

The challenge to be with each baby seemed to set a precedent. The two children battle for his attention.

Fascinated, we'd watch the babies as one crawler would immediately notice if the other climbed onto Pepa's lap. As fast as their little body could move, the youngster would wriggle across the room to claim their spot.

As they became sturdier on their feet, the competition heated up. If one of the toddlers decided the other was getting too much play time with their grandfather, they would either shove their adversary aside or yank them back by the hair on their head.

The pushes, whimpers, and periodical temper tantrums

have developed over time to more sophisticated ploys to distract the opponent and win Pepa's affection. In grade school now, their strategies fittingly engage their particular skills.

Ryan's strength is action. Pictures capture the intensity on his face as he's run down the soccer field and lined up his foot with the ball for the kick. He rides his bike fast and then skids to a stop. He skips rocks across the water five and six hops at a time.

He says, "Look what I can do, Pepa." A cock of his eyebrow and smug smile say *I can out do you, Emercyn.*

Emercyn's strength is capturing the moment. She adjusts her catcher's knee pads perfectly and waves to the crowd as she exits the softball field. She places her hand on her hip and tilts her foot to show off her stylish choice of shoes. She sighs and tells Ryan that she could skip rocks if she wanted to.

She says, "Look at me, Pepa." Her raised eyebrow and nod say *I'm a force to be reckoned with, Ryan.*

On more than one occasion, they've come to me with little worry lines on their foreheads, wondering where Pepa went. I assure them that he will be back shortly. As soon as he arrives, they run to him. Why not? Pepa has a tractor. Pepa buys candy. But mostly, Pepa is devoted to their every need.

All their energy goes to gain his attention.

There's no doubt they will continue to adore their Pepa, and I'm sure the battle for recognition will resolve itself as they learn that there is plenty of their grandfather to go around.

That's how our relationship with God should be. He is thrilled that we are his children. He watches us with pleasure, and he loves when we invest all our strength and abilities to make him happy.

Receiving God's Word

"Exult in his holy name; rejoice, you who worship the Lord. Search for the Lord and for his strength; continually seek him."

I Chronicles 16:10-11

Connecting with God's Word

Where should we look for strength?

Responding to God's Word

Is there anything you want to say to God?

Strength

What truth about strength can you relate to today?

Day 4 - STRENGTH

Be Aware

It's important to remember that our strength is entirely dependent on God.

"If you think you are standing strong, be careful not to fall. The temptations in your life are no different from what others experience. And God is faithful. He will not allow the temptation to be more than you can stand. When you are tempted, he will show you a way out so that you can endure."

I Corinthians 10:12-13

The Bible gives us instructions on how to trust God for our strength.

1. The book of Deuteronomy says we don't have to fear because God goes before us. Read *Deuteronomy 31:6.*

2. The book of I Timothy says God trusts us to do what he asks. Read *I Timothy 1:12.*

~Strength Knowledge~

God's words will tell you how to stand firm.

Receiving God's Word

"But the Lord stood with me and gave me strength so that I might preach the Good News in its entirety for all the Gentiles to hear. And he rescued me from certain death. Yes, and the Lord will deliver me from every evil attack and will bring me safely into his heavenly Kingdom. All glory to God forever and ever! Amen."

II Timothy 4:17-18

Connecting with God's Word

Do Christ-Followers ever stand alone?

Responding to God's Word

Is there anything you want to say to God?

Strength

What truth about strength can you relate to today?

Day 5 - STRENGTH

Understand

Receiving God's Word

Do you need God's plan for obedient strength? "God is our refuge and strength, always ready to help in times of trouble."

Psalm 46:1

Why do you need God's plan for strength? "This is what the Lord says: 'Cursed are those who put their trust in mere humans, who rely on human strength and turn their hearts away from the Lord.'"

Jeremiah 17:5

What is God's plan for strength? "When we were utterly helpless, Christ came at just the right time and died for us sinners."

Romans 5:6

What is my part in God's plan for strength? "See, God has come to save me. I will trust in him and not be afraid. The Lord God is my strength and my song; he has given me victory."

Isaiah 12:2

Will God's plan for strength work for me? "Don't be afraid, for I am with you. Don't be discouraged, for I am your God. I will strengthen you and help you. I will hold you up with my victorious right hand. "See, all your angry enemies lie there, confused and humiliated. Anyone who opposes you will die and come to nothing."

Isaiah 41:10-11

How can I know God's plan worked for me? "He will keep you strong to the end so that you will be free from all blame on the day when our Lord Jesus Christ returns. God will do this, for he is faithful to do what he says, and he has invited you into partnership with his Son, Jesus Christ our Lord."

I Corinthians 1:8-9

Connecting with God's Word

Is God's plan with you dependent on his strength or yours?

Responding to God's Word

Is there anything you want to say to God?

Strength

What truth about strength can you relate to today?

Day 6 - STRENGTH

The Test

Strength dictates how God sees us. The Bible says God's eyes search the earth to strengthen his people. Read *II Chronicles 16:9.*

Strength dictates God's focus. As soon as we pray, God answers and strengthens. Read *Psalm 138:3.*

Strength changes how we see ourselves. We have a spirit of power, love and self-discipline. Read *II Timothy 1:7.*

Strength changes our daily lives. We use God's strength in the gifts he assigns us to help others. Read *I Peter 4:10-11.*

Receiving God's Word

"The Lord is my strength and shield. I trust him with all my heart. He helps me, and my heart is filled with joy. I burst out in songs of thanksgiving. The Lord gives his people strength. He is a safe fortress for his anointed king."

Psalm 28:7-8

Connecting with God's Word

Do you trust God's strength in your life?

Responding to God's Word

Is there anything you want to say to God?

Strength

What truth about strength can you relate to today?

Day 7 - STRENGTH

The Experience

When the wind picks up, the eagle isn't concerned. The bird's innate reasoning says to lift from its vertical sitting position and spread its resting feathers.

As the wind accelerates, the fowl's wings stretch out further, pulling the bird to an entirely horizontal position.

Any fierce gale merely gives the eagle occasion to show its grandeur. It was created to fly!

With ease, the masterfully made bird swoops into the wind and glides. The stronger the force, the higher it soars.

"But those who trust in the Lord will find new strength. They will soar high on wings like eagles. They will run and not grow weary. They will walk and not faint."

Isaiah 40:31

God wants us to see life's circumstances as opportunities to show the breadth of his goodness. We too can soar and reach new heights, if we remember the Almighty's strength is carrying us.

Receiving God's Word

"I can do all things through Christ which strengtheneth me."

Philippians 4:13

Connecting with God's Word

What are my limitations?

Responding to God's Word

Is there anything you want to say to God?

Strength

What truth about strength can you relate to today?

Melissa Kirk

Dear Lord,

Thank you for giving me strength. I pray I will always use what you give me to glorify you. I trust you as my safe fortress.

Amen

Melissa Kirk

Embracing the Edict

Heart. Soul. Mind. Strength.

A lovely bowl graces the table, filled with chunks of Gala apples tossed in a crisp Waldorf salad. Next to it sits a hot Granny apple pie waiting to be sliced. Rich caramel coated Jonathan apples pierced with a stick and rolled in crushed peanuts line the counter next to the stove where a pan of blended Baldwin and Winesap apples simmers, filling the 4oom with a mouthwatering aroma.

Chosen from the harvest for their strong core, seed, flesh, and stem, each different apple variety bursts with flavor and the combined results is a lavish banquet. Just as God intended.

"And you must love the LORD your God with all your heart, all your soul, all your mind, and all your strength.' The second is equally important: 'Love your neighbor as yourself.' No other commandment is greater than these."

Mark 12:30-31

After a fresh look at the King's Edict, I've had to ask myself the questions I asked you at the beginning.

What's under my skin? Is my heart pulsating in eager anticipation for God's next move? Is my soul prioritizing him over everything? Is my mind thinking of ways to expand the kingdom's exposure? Is my every ounce of being pursuing him?

As a Christ-Follower, it's my prayer that, with all of my heart, soul, mind, and strength, I will want to contribute to the banquet God is planning. I pray you will desire the same.

READ MORE

Melissa Kirk

GROUP DISCUSSION NOTES

For success, be sure to plan ahead. Invite participants to the study. Conduct the meetings when it is most convenient for the group. Give attendees the book and assign the introduction and the first topic, "Heart", to be completed before the first meeting. Set up everything for each meeting before the starting time. Review the week's discussion and when possible, enlist volunteers in advance for scripture readings. Keep the meeting short – an hour and one-half or less is plenty. Most important, keep it simple.

In advance: Prepare a poster board or dry erase board that has Mark 12:29-31 written on it. Use any Bible translation of the verse that works for your group. The following is from the New Living Translation:

"Jesus replied, "The most important commandment is this: 'Listen, O Israel! The Lord our God is the one and only Lord. And you must love the Lord your God with all your heart, all your soul, all your mind, and all your strength.' The second is equally important: 'Love your neighbor as yourself.' No other commandment is greater than these."

Mark 12:29-31

Prepare a display that includes a variety of apples or apple pictures and the poster board. It should be within easy reach of the leader.

Optional activities to include in your meetings:

› Refreshments. Decide if you will serve refreshments at the beginning or after the group discussion. Keep it consistent if possible. Apple based recipes would be great!

› Have participants bring an item for the local food bank, nursing home, or children's home, etc. each week and assign someone to deliver the contributions after the final meeting.

› Ask volunteers in advance to do an activity. Examples are:
· Sing a hymn or lead the group in a song that fits the theme.
· Read a poem that fits the weekly theme.
· Watch a short YouTube video about the week's topic.
· Give a personal testimony.
· Lead a craft time that takes no more than fifteen minutes.

NOTE: Volunteers should have everything ready before the meeting begins so there won't be non-constructive down time.

ALSO: Door prizes are always fun.

Melissa Kirk

WEEK ONE – HEART

Welcome everyone and allow time for introductions if necessary.

1. Point to the display and say, "For the next four weeks, we will work to memorize *Mark 12:29-31*. These scripture verses will remind us that God has issued an edict between him and us. It pertains to every part of our life. Each week, we will recite the verses, and then remove one-quarter of the scripture. By the end of our last meeting, we will be able to recite it from memory. As a group, read *Mark 12:29-31* from the poster board.

Open in prayer.

2. Heart – In Worship

   Responsive Reading: As a group, read aloud the first page of "In Worship" for the week of *Heart*. The leader reads the words in bold letters followed by the group responding with the text. Enlist two participants to be prepared to read the included scriptures.

3. Any prearranged volunteer music, reading, or video would be appropriate now. However, any craft activity time would be better after group discussion.

4. Heart – The Outpouring

   Say "Hannah poured out her heart to God. What did she offer him? Do you think it was an appropriate offering? Why or why not?" Allow for discussion.

5. Heart – All In

   Say "Have you ever been involved in a project where everyone worked together to honor God? What was it like?" Allow for discussion.

6. Heart – Be Aware

Ask for a volunteer to read *Proverbs 21:2.*

Say "Our definition of heart is 'where interests thrive.' What does that mean to you? Has your heart every misguided you? What did it feel like?" Allow for discussion.

7. Heart – Understand

Say "After becoming a Christ-Follower, our heart will still deceive us. What are some steps you can do to keep your heart centered on God?" Allow for discussion.

8. Heart – The Test

Say "If our heart is obedient, we will recognize God's direction. What is something we can do to keep our heart in line with his will?" Allow for discussion.

9. Heart – The Experience

Ask for a volunteer to read *I John 1:9.*

What did you related to most with David's story?" What should we do when we sin against God?" Allow for discussion.

Say "Your assignment this week is to think about a way you can obey God with your heart and study the topic of "Soul."

10. Prearranged volunteer crafts are appropriate here.

WEEK TWO – SOUL

Welcome everyone and allow time for introductions if necessary.

1. Point to the display and say, "We are memorizing *Mark 12:29-31*. These scripture verses will remind us that God has issued an edict between him and us that pertains to every area of our life. As a group, read *Mark 12:29-31* from the board. Erase or mark out one-fourth of the words and repeat saying it.

   Open in prayer.

2. Soul – In Worship

Responsive Reading: As a group, read aloud the first page of "In Worship" for the week of *Soul*. The leader reads the words in bold letters followed by the group responding with the text. Enlist two participants to be prepared to read the included scriptures.

3. Any prearranged volunteer music, reading, or video would be appropriate now. However, any craft activity time would be better after group discussion.

4. Soul – Crying Out

   Say "The Psalmist cried out in despair. Which of his observations was most meaningful to you? Why?" Allow for discussion.

5. Soul – Security

   Say "How important is it to allow God to carry the burdens of your life? Do you trust him with your soul? Why or why not?" Allow for discussion.

6. Soul – Be Aware

   Ask for a volunteer to read *Jeremiah 6:16.*

   Say "Have you every decided your way was the best way? How did it end?" Allow for discussion.

7. Soul – Understand

   Say "What is the hardest thing for you to give up for God?" Allow for discussion.

8. Soul – The Test

   Say "How do you feel knowing God protects you? Do you ever feel unsafe?" Allow for discussion.

9. Soul – The Experience

   Ask for a volunteer to read *Luke 16:22-26*.

   Say "Do you think we concern ourselves enough with the souls of others? Why or why not?" Allow for discussion.

   Say "Your assignment this week is to discover a new way to remember your soul's connection to God and study the topic of "Mind."

10. Prearranged volunteer crafts are appropriate here.

Melissa Kirk

WEEK THREE – MIND

Welcome everyone and allow time for introductions if necessary.

1. Point to the display and say, "We are memorizing *Mark 12:29-31.* These scripture verses will remind us that God has issued an edict between him and us that pertains to every area of our life.

   As a group, read *Mark 12:29-31* from the board. Erase or mark out one-half of the words and repeat saying it. Open in prayer.

2. Mind – In Worship

Responsive Reading: As a group, read aloud the first page of "In Worship" for the week of *Mind*. The leader reads the words in bold letters followed by the group responding with the text. Enlist two participants to be prepared to read the included scriptures.

3. Any prearranged volunteer music, reading, or video would be appropriate now. However, any craft activity time would be better after group discussion.

4. Mind – Searching

   Say "King Solomon searched for the meaning of life. What did he compare the search to? Which of his observations bother you the most? Why?" Allow for discussion.

5. Mind – One Mind

   Say "What is something you do or wish that you did to help others have a unified mind with God?" Allow for discussion.

6. Mind – Be Aware

   Ask for a volunteer to read *Romans 1:28.*

   Say "Does this verse disturb you? If so, how? If not, why? " Allow for discussion.

7. Mind – Understand

   Say "What types of things would you like for God to help you understand?" Allow for discussion.

8. Mind – The Test

   Say "What are some steps we can take to ensure that the Holy Spirit controls our mind?" Allow for discussion.

9. Mind – The Experience

   Ask for a volunteer to read *I Peter 1:13-16.*

   Say "Peter often spoke without thinking. Some people never bother to speak up. Do you think one action is worse or better than the other? Why?" Allow for discussion.

   Say "Your assignment this week is to look for a special scripture verse that you will read when you realize your mind is under attack and study the topic of "Strength."

10. Prearranged volunteer crafts are appropriate here.

Melissa Kirk

WEEK FOUR – STRENGTH

Welcome everyone and allow time for introductions if necessary.

1. Point to the display and say, "We have been memorizing *Mark 12:29-31*. These scripture verses reminds us that God has issued an edict between him and us that pertains to every area of our life.

   As a group, read *Mark 12:29-31* from the board. Remove the board and repeat the verse. Congratulate the group for their hard work.

Open in prayer.

2. Strength – In Worship

   Responsive Reading: As a group, read aloud the first page of "In Worship" for the week of *Strength*. The leader reads the words in bold letters followed by the group responding with the text. Enlist two participants to be prepared to read the included scriptures.

3. Any prearranged volunteer music, reading, or video would be appropriate now. However, any craft activity time would be better after group discussion.

4. Strength – Misdirected Life

   Say "Samson had incredible strength. He wasted and abused it. But in the end, God's will was done. Have you ever felt you wasted something God gave you, but then witness him fulfill his plan anyway? Would you like to share the experience?" Allow for discussion.

5. Strength – Full Focus

   Say "How important is it to please God? What happens if we don't?" Allow for discussion.

6. Strength – Be Aware

   Ask for a volunteer to read *I Corinthians 10:12-13.*

Ask for a volunteer to read *II Timothy 4:17-18*.

Say "Can a person avoid all temptations? Can they overcome temptations? How?" Allow for discussion.

7. Strength – Understand

   Say "What will happen to God's enemies? How does that give you strength?" Allow for discussion.

8. Strength – The Test

   Say "What does a spirit of power feel like?" Allow for discussion.

9. Strength – The Experience

   Ask for a volunteer to read *Isaiah 40:31*.

   Say "The eagle isn't concerned with the wind because God created it to fly. God says we can soar high and not grow weary. What is a practical step you can take to trust God for strength?" Allow for discussion.

10. Prearranged volunteer crafts are appropriate here.

Melissa Kirk

Excerpt

GRACE WARRIOR
Bathed in Mercy, Clothed in Grace
Grace Warrior Devotional Series

Melissa Kirk

Grace Warrior

If you are my sibling-in-Christ, then I know you've experienced the mercy of God. He met you at the cross. He stripped off the dirty, ugly, often tattered and worn-out life clothes, and as Psalm 103 says, he removed those rags as far as the east is from the west. At that moment, you became clean. And vulnerable.

I don't do clean well. By the end of the day, I will have evidence of everything I've eaten, and a lot of what I've said, all over me. Vulnerable? When I find myself in unknown territory, I suddenly feel inadequate.

Mercy removed our guilt, but clean and vulnerable sounds hard, doesn't it? Well, we can thank God that he didn't stop with just mercy. What else happened at the cross?

Rest assured, we didn't catch the Almighty off guard.

God told the prophet, Jeremiah, that before he ever formed him in his mother's womb, he gave him an appointment.

Us too! God had a good and perfect will for each of us before we were ever born. What is your purpose? What is his plan for you? You may not have it titled or thought much about it, but you know at least a little. You can probably think of times when you were poked or prodded in a different direction. Maybe you remember a time being squeezed or molded into a different thought pattern. Or perhaps, you've had a barrier thrown up on one of life's paths while an entire wall collapsed on another.

That's divine direction and holy intervention. God's plan for you is in full motion, and it's invading every part of your life.

What if, at the cross, God had said, "Welcome to the family! I've got a chore for you. Good luck with that." Huh? He didn't. No, what God did when he bathed you in mercy, was to immediately clothe you in grace.

You are now dressed in the best. Those ugly and tattered rags are gone! Marvelous grace adorns you.

Do you know what the most amazing, priceless thing about your new *grace* clothes is? They will always fit you. Grace will dress you for every occasion in your life. Every situation!

God told Paul, "My grace is all you need. My power works best in weakness." Paul's weaknesses could have been physical ailments, or the authorities questioning his apostleship, or a combination of many things.

For you – whether your weakness is a limitation you've allowed yourself, or a constraint that someone else has placed on you, know that you are just like Paul. God has an endless supply of grace. Where you are weak, he is all powerful.

Friend, at the cross, he gave you mercy, purpose, and grace to fulfill that purpose. He is the King. You are his child. He's given you a task specifically designed for you; that only your shoes are meant to fill.

If you haven't experienced the mercy of God, this book will encourage and guide you to a better understanding of God's desire for you.

To my siblings-in-Christ, I hope you will consider what your purpose in God's plan is. Most important, I pray you will daily recognize God's grace and its potential through you.

God gave me mercy, purpose, and grace. Admittedly, I'm a work in progress. I'm Melissa Kirk, *grace warrior*. My task is to encourage you to rise with me as a warrior for the Kingdom, bathed in mercy, clothed in grace.

Excerpt

ADVENT

Celebrate the Coming

Grace Warrior Devotional Series

Melissa Kirk

Advent

In years past, the chaotic, commercialized, celebration of Christmas sucked the life out of me. I love Christmas!

But, there's the *Final Sales Event of the Season* that happens every weekend. Charity drives, company socials, family dinners, parades, church plays, and band concerts fill the calendar. Apparently sleep isn't necessary the last six weeks of the year.

Christmas decorations crowding out pumpkins before the first leaf falls bugs me. Happy Holidays versus Merry Christmas debates on social media are annoying. One

Christmas carol per sixty Santa Baby songs on the radio bothers me. And, the Babe-in-a-manger piece haphazardly stuffed between a Ninja Turtle Cowabunga Christmas plaque and a snow globe with Frosty in beachwear sends me over the edge.

For years, I lit up the entire house with twinkling lights. Bah humbug putting that mess away. Once, I did the reverse and simplified. No one appreciated the oranges, apples, and walnuts in their stocking.

My strategies weren't working, but with three children, eleven grandchildren, and a great-grandchild, a full retreat wasn't an option. So, I had a conversation with God after the last yuletide, and through a summer of reflection, I realized the problem. I was misinterpreting the season's rules of engagement. Until now, my battle cry was:

It's Christmas. I will survive.
I will decorate my home fashionably. It's Christmas.
I will prepare a large family meal. It's Christmas.
I will buy lots of presents. It's Christmas.
I will insist everyone experience peace and goodwill or else!
It's Christmas. I will survive.

I had it wrong, and my life was void of all that the Advent season celebrated: hope, peace, joy, and love.

God reminded me that the world's idea of celebration contradicts his, but it's *his* battle, not mine.

He reiterated that Christmas doesn't stop people from hurting. It doesn't take away restlessness or discouragement or loneliness. Hope, peace, joy and love so desperately sought after is found in Christ alone; not in the celebration.

He requested I recall my rank. You may have noticed a whole lot of *I's* in the above thoughts. He did too. God wants my participation in his kingdom affairs, *under* his authority.

So, you'll still find me in the midst of the chaotic, commercialized, celebration of Christmas, but hopefully a new me; with a clearer understanding of God's seasonal rules of engagement. My duty as a grace warrior for the kingdom is to follow his simple directives: converse and share.

When my hands dig through the sixty percent off pile of pajamas, hope can be shared by buying a set for the children's shelter and praying for the child who wears them. While waiting in line behind the young couple who is trying to decide if they can afford the milk, diapers, *and* discounted plastic toy truck, peace can be shared by slipping a ten dollar bill their way and inviting them to the free church community meal. Joy can be shared by reciting a few lines from *The Magnificat* with a new mother. As the community parade floats pass by, love can be shared by telling the person standing next to me about God's faithfulness. Here's my new battle cry.

God sent his Son, Jesus. He is coming again, soon.
God sent a star to light our way. Celebrate and share hope.
God's heavenly hosts cried out. Celebrate and share peace.
God's gift is eternal life. Celebrate and share joy.
God's gift is available to all. Celebrate and share love.
God sent his Son, Jesus. He is coming again, soon.

Whether your Advent season is packed with festivities, or mostly alone time, God's directives are the same: converse and share.

The gifts people want are your time, your smile, your touch, and most importantly, your testimony of the celebration *you* have because you received God's gift of eternal life; free from death and decay.

If you haven't accepted his gift, my prayer is that you'll have a personal conversation with the Almighty. It's because of his Son; we celebrate the Advent season.

Thank you

Thank you to my fellow Christian Communicators: Cary Sanchez, Beth Saadati, Bobbie Frazier, Julie Dykes, Angela Holston, Jan Willis, Jerri Marr, and Naomi R. Shedd. Your testimonials are very dear to me. They communicate your personalities beautifully.

Thank you to the rest of my family and friends for your encouraging words.

And a very special thank you to my husband, Larry, who took our dog, Mert, on extra-long walks so I could write in peace.

Thank you to my readers. I wish you the very best in all seasons of your life.

To follow my Grace Warrior blog, kindly visit www.MelissaKirk.ORG and subscribe to receive e-mail notifications. I promise not to flood your inboxes.

Special Links

Grace Warrior Blog

www.MelissaKirk.ORG or www.TheGraceWarrior.com

Facebook - Personal

 Melissa C Kirk

Facebook – Author

MelissaKirkAuthor

Pinterest

MelissaCKirk

Twitter

@melissackirk

Google +

Melissa C Kirk Grace Warrior

Instagram

Melissackirk

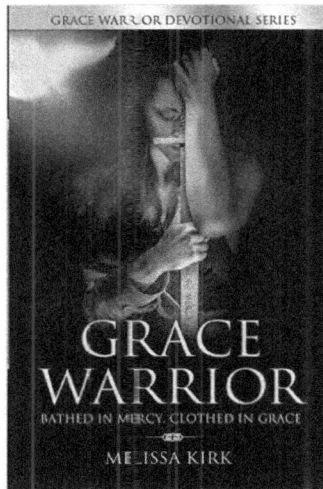

Grace Warrior – *Bathed in Mercy, Clothed in Grace*

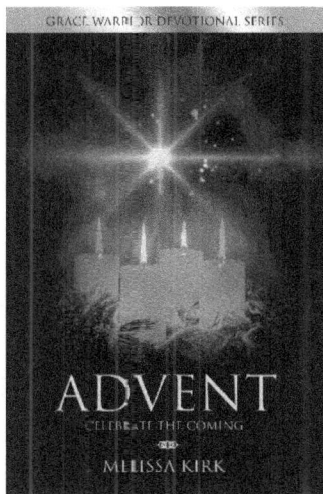

Advent – *Celebrate the Coming*

www.MelissaKirk.ORG   or   www.Amazon.com

Go in God's Grace

www.ingramcontent.com/pod-product-compliance
Lightning Source LLC
Chambersburg PA
CBHW020502030426
42337CB00011B/202

* 9 7 8 0 9 9 6 9 2 3 1 2 5 *